TO DO JUSTICE AND TO LOVE MERCY

An Introduction to Catholic Social Teaching

WORKBOOK

TO DO JUSTICE AND TO LOVE MERCY

An Introduction to Catholic Social Teaching

WORKBOOK

TAN Books
Gastonia, NC

Series design by Margaret Ryland

Cover and layout by Caroline Green

Cover image: Jesus and the Woman Taken in Adultery, 1577, Alessandro Allori. Luisa Ricciarini / Bridgeman Images.

ISBN: 978-1-5051-1819-3

Published in the United States by
TAN Books
PO Box 269
Gastonia, NC 28053
www.TANBooks.com

Printed in the United States of America

Contents

A Note to Instructors

As Pope St. John Paul II made clear in his apostolic exhortation *Catechesi Tradendae*, "The definitive aim of catechesis is to put people not only in touch but in communion, in intimacy, with Jesus Christ."

The *Formed in Christ* series seeks to fulfill this call, fostering intimacy with Christ through its dynamic content.

Rather than presenting religion as any other subject to be mastered, our series editors have designed each text to plumb the bottomless genius of Catholicism found in centuries of theologians, saints, councils, and papal teachings.

The six volumes in *Formed in Christ* cover every point in the USCCB's guidelines for high school catechesis, while the five electives in the series further complement the material.

Catholics are called not only to be holy in their private lives, but to live out their faith in the public square. But just what does it look like to live as a Catholic in the world? *To Do Justice and to Love Mercy: An Introduction to Catholic Social Teaching* shows not only the *how* but the *why* of Catholic social teaching.

As a thorough and orthodox outlining of the principles proclaimed by Holy Mother Church, this book dives into God's plan for every person's happiness, examines the nature of sin and its social dimensions, as well as how the Ten Commandments and the Beatitudes guide our life in community, and just what charity and justice should look like today. With an appendix on commonly held objections and questions about the social teachings of the Church, *To Do Justice and to Love Mercy* teaches people of all ages and backgrounds just how God intended his people to live in society.

This supplemental workbook is designed to provide instructors with test material and direction for enhancing students' grasp of the material.

For each chapter, the following components are included:

Memory Verse

Appealing not only to the head but also the heart, a suitable memory verse, chosen for its relation to the chapter's content, is suggested to help students with their prayer life. Throughout the week, have your student attempt to recite this verse from memory.

Key Terms

A list of key terms from the chapter is included. Students are encouraged to write down some notes about these terms (either here in the workbook or in a separate notebook), using not only the text but the *Catechism of the Catholic Church* and a good Catholic dictionary as well. This will not only prepare students for testing but deepen their understanding of the content.

Questions for Review

Taken directly from the student text, the Questions for Review, provided in "short answer" format, ensure comprehension of the material. Answers are provided in the back.

Quiz

For each chapter, ten questions are provided for testing. Multiple Choice, True or False, and Fill-in-the-Blank quizzes vary throughout the workbook. Answers are provided in the back.

Questions for Discussion

Dialogue between students and instructors is essential. Not only will the Questions for Discussion (included both here and in the student text) provide another opportunity for reinforcing the material, but the questions are specifically designed to prompt students to reflect on their own faith experience. While discussion between students and instructors is highly recommended, the Questions for Discussion can also be used as prompts for personal writing exercises. Since these are more for personal reflection, no answers are provided.

Essay Topics and/or Further Study

The *Formed in Christ* series is designed to expose students to Church documents and the writings of theologians from all stages of Church history. But these selected readings are just the beginning of Catholic thought that students can discover. The Essay Topics and/or Further Study suggestions encourage students to dig deeper into the wealth of Catholic teaching through independent study. A mix of personal, subjective prompts and research topics, these suggestions will enable students to learn more about their Catholic faith. Grading is left up to the instructor's discretion.

Final Exam

In the back, you will find a final exam that aggregates all the most important content. This provides a barometer for how well your student(s) absorbed the material. It consists of matching and short answer. Answers are provided in the back.

Part I

God's Plan for His People

Part I: Chapter 1

The Call of God

Memory Verse

> No longer do I call you servants, for the servant does not know what his master is doing; but I have called you friends, for all that I have heard from my Father I have made known to you. You did not choose me, but I chose you and appointed you that you should go and bear fruit and that your fruit should abide; so that whatever you ask the Father in my name, he may give it to you. This I command you, to love one another.

—John 15:15–17

Key Terms

Original sin

Hell

Paschal mystery

Questions for Review

1. What is the call of Jesus that is reflected in Catholic social teaching?

2. What is hell?

3. Why do we need someone divine to save us?

4. Why do we need someone human to save us?

5. What is the paschal mystery?

Quiz

True / False

1. ____ The primary way to view the Catholic faith is as a set of rules and laws we must follow to get to heaven.
2. ____ The Church's teachings on social issues reflect the love we are supposed to have for Jesus Christ as seen through concrete actions to help and love our neighbors.
3. ____ As much as we might think we are able to, we cannot save ourselves because of sin; we must have someone divine to save us and forgive our sins.
4. ____ In his death, Jesus took on the consequences of our sins and transformed them.
5. ____ The passion, death, resurrection, and ascension of Jesus Christ is called the paschal mystery.

Questions for Discussion

1. What are some of the ways you've seen people try to distract themselves from suffering? Have you tried to distract yourself from suffering? If so, how? Has it worked?
2. What is one way your actions have become an obstacle to your own happiness?
3. Have you ever tried to help someone but failed? What happened? Why were your efforts not successful?

Essay Topics / Further Study

1. Pretend that one of your non-religious friends says that he would never want to be Catholic because of all the rules of the faith and how that restricts your freedom and your ability to have fun. What would you say to refute this and explain the truth of the Catholic faith?
2. How would you explain to someone who asked you why Jesus had to become man to save us, rather than just remaining a divine being?
3. What is it about your Catholic faith that makes you want to go out and help and serve others?

Part I: Chapter 2

Happiness in This Life

Memory Verse

> Go therefore and make disciples of all nations, baptizing them in the name of the Father and of the Son and of the Holy Spirit, teaching them to observe all that I have commanded you; and behold, I am with you always, to the close of the age.
>
> —Matthew 28:19–20

Key Terms

The Family of God

The Great Commission

Questions for Review

1. What does it mean that we are created in God's image?

2. Who is our model for how we ought to live together in community?

3. Can we be perfectly happy on our own? Why or why not?

4. How do we become God's sons and daughters?

5. What is the most powerful encounter we can have with Jesus in this lifetime?

Quiz

1. Many people wrongly believe happiness is based on:
   A. reason.
   B. feelings and emotions.
   C. being with others.
2. Our happiness in this life requires that we are in communion with God and that we have:
   A. communion with our neighbors.
   B. communion with a spouse.
   C. communion with the natural world.
3. The family of God is:
   A. the saints and angels.
   B. all of humanity.
   C. the Church, the Body of Christ.
4. Christ left us his Church primarily so that:
   A. we could serve others.
   B. we could come to know and love him.
   C. we could better understand ourselves and the world around us.
5. Which sacraments let us know beyond a shadow of a doubt that Jesus loves us and wants us to be with him?
   A. Baptism, Marriage, and Holy Orders
   B. Baptism, Eucharist, and Confirmation
   C. Baptism, Eucharist, and Reconciliation

Questions for Discussion

1. What is something that you longed for and thought would make you completely happy in a lasting way? Did it?
2. What have been some of your happiest moments? Have you ever experienced being just a little bit sad, even in the midst of great happiness? If so, why do you think this happened?
3. Describe a time when you have felt particularly close to God. How was that happiness like other happy moments in your life? How was it different?

Essay Topics / Further Study

1. Name three areas of society where people constantly pursue happiness, only to be left unfulfilled. How would you show or explain to someone that these things will never truly bring happiness? Be specific.
2. Why do you think true happiness can only be found by being in communion with God, with his Church, and with our neighbors? Can you give examples from your own life that show this to be true? As you reflect on this, consider the difference between long-lasting joy and the fleeting pleasures of earthly things.
3. Does it help you understand the nature and purpose of the Church when you think of it as God's family on earth? How do you see the dynamics of your own family playing out in the wider family of God's Church? What similarities do you see?

Part II

The Roots and Development of Catholic Social Teaching

Part II: Chapter 1

The Church Has Always Stood for Charity and Justice

Memory Verse

> "Lord, when did we see thee hungry or thirsty or a stranger or naked or sick or in prison, and did not minister to thee?" Then he will answer them, "Truly, I say to you, as you did it not to one of the least of these, you did it not to me." And they will go away into eternal punishment, but the righteous into eternal life.
>
> —Matthew 25:45–46

Key Terms

Torah

The Ten Commandments

Anawim

The Sermon on the Mount

Our Father

The parable of the last judgment

Corporal works of mercy

Spiritual works of mercy

Questions for Review

1. What did the prophets urge the ancient Israelites to do?

2. Name three commandments from the Old Testament and describe how Jesus intensified each commandment.

3. Describe two ways the behavior of the early Christians differed from their pagan neighbors.

4. What are the corporal works of mercy?

5. What are the spiritual works of mercy?

Quiz

1. For the Church, charity and justice are not ____________.

2. God had to form his people and teach them in his ways through the __________, or "the law."

3. Because of their sins, God sent ___________ to remind the Israelites of his commandments and to warn them about the consequences of their actions.

4. In his _______________, Jesus elevated and intensified God's commandments.

5. In his ministry and teachings, Jesus showed us that we must do more than just __________ follow God's commands; we must follow them in our hearts as well.

6. The ____________ is the privileged prayer for Christians because it is the only prayer that Jesus himself taught us.

7. Jesus makes it clear that at the end of our lives, we will be judged by ____________.

8. The concept of ____________—the idea that every person has value by virtue of being human—was completely foreign to the ancient Greeks and Romans.

9. The __________ works of mercy are ways we can serve the bodily needs of our neighbor.

10. The __________ works of mercy are ways we can serve the spiritual needs of our neighbor.

Questions for Discussion

1. Do you see any differences between how faithful Christians behave today and how people who don't believe in God or don't actively practice their faith behave? If so, explain.
2. Who is someone that you know who lives the faith in an attractive, compelling way? What does this person do that makes him or her different from other people?
3. How do you think a failure to practice what we claim to believe undermines our witness in the culture? What difference do you think it would make if more people truly lived their faith?

Essay Topics / Further Study

1. Charity and justice are not usually two things you would think go together. Explain what each is and show how they work together to bring salvation to each of us. Specifically, reflect on how carrying out justice might actually be a charitable act.
2. Pick out several of the commandments and explain how Jesus enhanced or intensified them with his teachings.
3. Pretend like you were present to hear Jesus's Sermon on the Mount, and you must write a letter to your cousin who was not there, telling him what Jesus said and what you think he meant by his teachings. What would you say in that letter?
4. Make a list of the corporal works of mercy and write down specific ways you can carry them out this week.
5. Make a list of the spiritual works of mercy and write down specific was you can carry them out this week.

Part II: Chapter 2

The Catholic Understanding of Justice

Memory Verse

> When justice is done, it is a joy to the righteous, but dismay to evildoers.
>
> —Proverbs 21:15

Key Terms

Justice

Legal justice

Distributive justice

Commutative justice

Social justice

Questions for Review

1. What are the four types of justice? Name and give a short definition for each.

2. What are three things political authorities owe to their citizens? What are three things citizen owe to political authorities?

3. Are people obliged to obey immoral laws? Why or why not?

4. What is the basis for all legitimate rights?

5. How are all people equal? How are they not equal? When are inequalities good, and when are they bad?

Quiz

True/False

1. ____ Catholic social teaching is rooted in Scripture.
2. ____ Justice is the moral virtue that demands sinners be punished for their sinful actions.
3. ____ Regardless of any teaching we may receive throughout our lives, we have an innate sense of justice that we are born with.
4. ____ Legal justice deals with matters in the political realm.
5. ____ The Church does not tell governments or citizens how to approach every single question of governance.
6. ____ A Catholic is not bound, and in fact must disobey, any law that conflicts with God's law.
7. ____ Citizens have the duty to obey political authorities, but those authorities have no duties to their citizens.
8. ____ Armed resistance is permission to a political authority, but only if certain conditions are met.
9. ____ Social justice can only exist if distributive and legal justice exist first.
10. ____ Certain inequalities can be a good thing because they show our dependence on one another.

Questions for Discussion

1. Can you think of an example of an unjust law? What are some ways you can work to change that law?
2. How does our culture promote human dignity? How does it undermine human dignity?
3. In your own life, what are some of the good things you have experienced from the differences that exist among your friends and family? What are some of the bad things you have seen result from inequality?

Essay Topics / Further Study

1. Some may incorrectly think that justice is all about enacting punishments on those who do wrong. How does it influence your understanding of justice to know it is actually defined as "giving to God and to others what is due to them?"
2. In the text it said that two kinds of justice—distributive and social—are particularly important in shaping Church teaching. Why do you think that is?
3. Give an example of an unjust law that you would have to disobey because it conflicts with God's law. Answer by way of a letter you write to your family from prison explaining the stance you are taking when they would rather you just obey and be a free person.
4. Explain how some inequalities in a society between its members can be a good thing or a bad thing. Give examples.

Part II: Chapter 3

Charity and Justice in the Modern Era

Memory Verse

> Render to Caesar the things that are Caesar's, and to God the things that are God's.
>
> —Mark 12:17

Key Terms

Encyclical

Rerum Novarum

Pacem in Terris

Quadragesimo Anno

Mater et Magistra

Populorum Progressio

Gaudium et Spes

Laborem Exercens

Sollicitudo Rei Socialis

Centesimus Annus

Evangelium Vitae

Catechism of the Catholic Church

USCCB

Compendium of the Social Doctrine of the Church

Caritas in Veritate

Laudato Si'

Questions for Review

1. What is considered the Church's first social encyclical? Who wrote it? When and why?

2. What social encyclical was written, in large part, to condemn racism and address issues surrounding the US civil rights movement? Who wrote this encyclical?

3. What social encyclical is dedicated to the right to life? Who wrote this encyclical?

4. What are the social encyclicals of Pope Benedict XVI and Pope Francis?

5. What three principles inform all of the social encyclicals of the Church?

Quiz

1. The advent of ______________ radically changed the social and economic fabric of much of the world.
   A. World War I
   B. the Civil Rights Movement
   C. the Industrial Revolution
2. Who wrote *Rerum Novarum* ("Of Revolutionary Change")?
   A. Pope Pius XI
   B. Pope Leo XIII
   C. Pope John Paul II
3. Which of the following is not one of the rights of workers as outlined in *Rerum Novarum*?
   A. the right to a living wage
   B. the right to not be forced to work unreasonably long hours
   C. the right to manage themselves
4. ______________ was the first social encyclical to address international poverty, as opposed to only addressing poverty in the Western developed world.
   A. *Mater et Magistra*
   B. *Rerum Novarum*
   C. *Pacem in Terris*
5. *Pacem in Terris* condemned all of the following except:
   A. racism.
   B. the arms race.
   C. pollution.
6. Who commissioned the creation of the *Catechism of the Catholic Church,* published in 1992?
   A. Pope Benedict XVI
   B. Pope John Paul II
   C. Pope John XXIII
7. Pope Francis's encyclical on caring for the environment is called:
   A. *Laudato Si'*
   B. *Caritas in Veritate*
   C. *Evangelium Vitae*
8. True or False: Pope Francis is the only modern pope to address environmental issues?
   A. True
   B. False

9. What provides the foundation for all social teaching?
   A. moral law
   B. civil law
   C. Church law

10. Who is the source of all civil authority?
    A. man
    B. God
    C. the United Nations

Questions for Discussion

1. Do you think the Church should comment on issues like the arms race or civil rights? Why or why not?
2. When you form your opinions about politics or current events, where do you go for information? Why?
3. To what extent does your faith shape how you think about politics and current events? Could it play a bigger role? Should it play a bigger role? Why or why not?

Essay Topics / Further Study

1. Pick one of the encyclicals from the text to study further. Read it online and make an outline of all its major points. Be sure to include the historical context in which it was written. What struck you as the most important aspects of it, and what were its greatest effects on the culture?
2. Write an "encyclical" for your family (and give it a cool Latin name!) that details all the issues that pop up in family life and how to best address them.
3. Pretend that a non-Catholic friend sends you an e-mail asking what the *Catechism of the Catholic Church* is, that he heard it mentioned somewhere and is curious as to what it is. How would you answer him? Give a brief history of how it came to be and what it aims to do.

Part III

Major Themes of Catholic Social Teaching

Part III: Chapter 1

The Cornerstone: The Dignity of Human Life

Memory Verse

> So God created man in his own image, in the image of God he created them.
>
> —Genesis 1:27

Key Terms

Anthropology

Materialistic anthropology

Dualistic anthropology

Hylomorphism

Personalistic principle

Questions for Review

1. What does the word "anthropology" mean?

2. What is a materialistic anthropology? What is a dualistic anthropology? What is wrong with both?

3. What is hylomorphism?

4. What is the personalistic principle?

5. In what ways does the human person image God?

Quiz

1. ______________ is foundational to the Christian understanding of the human person and how we are to live.

2. Some people say that human beings are no more than highly intelligent __________, made up exclusively of cells, synapses, and metabolic processes.

3. Those who believe that the soul and body are separate and that the soul is all that matters are known as __________.

4. Christian anthropology sees the body as __________ in that it is a visible manifestation of the deeper spiritual reality within us.

5. Though we are made in the image of God, __________ can distort that image.

Questions for Discussion

1. Can you think of a way our culture promotes a dualistic or materialistic anthropology? Explain.
2. You were created in the image of God. What does this tell you about how you should treat yourself? Can you give an example of a way you have not treated yourself with the proper respect?
3. Every person you meet is created in the image of God. What does this tell you about how you should treat others? Can you give an example of a way you or someone close to you has not treated someone else with the proper respect?

Essay Topics / Further Study

1. Pretend you are in a round table discussion with two people: one who subscribes to the materialistic view of anthropology and the other the dualistic. How would you convince each that he was wrong?
2. What do you think it means when the text says Christian anthropology sees the body as *sacramental*?
3. Read the selected reading from Pope St. John Paul II concerning *Evangelium Vitae*. What are the main points he is making in this excerpt?

Part III: Chapter 2

Building Blocks

Memory Verse

> If any one says, "I love God," and hates his brother, he is a liar; for he who does not love his brother whom he has seen, cannot love God whom he has not seen. And this commandment we have from him, that he who loves God should love his brother also.
>
> —1 John 4:20–21

Key Terms

Domestic church

Subsidiarity

Questions for Review

1. What institution is the foundation of all society?

2. What are four things just governments must ensure for all men and women regarding the family?

3. What makes for true community?

4. What are the three levels of participation in society to which each person is called?

5. Define "subsidiarity."

Quiz

True/False

1. ____ How we organize our society—in economics and politics, in law and policy—directly affects human dignity.
2. ____ The individual person is the foundation of society.
3. ____ The family unit forms the "domestic church," the basic building block of the Church universal, and the first school of faith, hope, and love for each of its members.
4. ____ The governments of the states seeking to control the federal government is an infringement on the practice of subsidiarity.
5. ____ The practice of subsidiarity should only be abandoned if outside help is necessary from a higher power.

Questions for Discussion

1. What are some of the lessons you've learned from your family that make you a good friend, a good student, and a good citizen?
2. When the family is broken and cannot care for children or form them in positive ways, what might happen—to individuals, society, and the government?
3. What are some ways you can fulfill your responsibilities to your family, community, and society at large?

Essay Topics / Further Discussion

1. Why do you think the Church teaches that the family is the foundation of society? Why would society only be as healthy as the health of its families?
2. Explain what the practice of subsidiarity is and give an example in everyday life. Why would it benefit society for issues and problems and daily life to be attended to by the "lower order" rather than the "higher order"?

Part III: Chapter 3

Essential Elements

Memory Verse

> Truly, I say to you, as you did it to one of the least of these my brethren, you did it to me.
>
> —Matthew 25:40

Key Terms

Preferential option for the poor

Centesimus Annus

Universal destination of goods

Spiritual poverty

Solidarity

Questions for Review

1. What does the Church mean by the phrase "preferential option for the poor"?

2. What is the "universal destination of goods"?

3. What basic rights of workers does the Church teach must be respected?

4. What is solidarity?

5. What is our obligation to creation?

Quiz

1. Anyone who cares for the poor:
   A. is guaranteed to enter heaven.
   B. establishes a relationship with Jesus.
   C. is considered a Christian.

2. The term "preferential option for the poor" means:
   A. the poor will enter heaven first.
   B. the poor have a right to the rich's goods.
   C. we must put the needs of the poor before our own needs.

3. The practice of ____________ says that we deserve to purchase and enjoy whatever we can afford with the money we have justly earned.
   A. consumerism
   B. capitalism
   C. communism

4. __________________ is not as easy to recognize or fix as material poverty, but it can be just as devastating (if not more) to human happiness.
   A. Emotional poverty
   B. Educational poverty
   C. Spiritual poverty

5. Which of the following is *not* one of the rights of workers recognized by the Church?
   A. the right to work from home to better manage family life
   B. the right to private property
   C. the right to form unions

Questions for Discussion

1. Do you think our society looks down on the poor? Why or why not? If so, why is this attitude wrongheaded?
2. What signs of spiritual poverty do you see in the world around you? What are some ways you can help alleviate spiritual poverty?
3. How do you think the Church's understanding of stewardship of creation is similar to secular environmentalism? How are they different? Which approach makes more sense to you and why?

Essay Topics / Further Discussion

1. Do research in your community to discover three ways you can serve the poor this week.
2. How would you explain the important and delicate balance between caring for the poor and the sharing of the earth's resources and the dangerous ideology of communism? How do you carry out the former without supporting the latter?
3. The text hints that spiritual poverty may cause more harm in the culture than material poverty. Do you agree? Why might this be so? Give examples.
4. There are examples of consumerism all throughout our society. Think back over the last several months and make a list of any time you have fallen victim to this mentality. What tangible things can you do to guard against the temptation to consumerism?
5. Make a list of three things you can do this week to care for the environment. Even though we must guard against the worship of nature, why do you think it is important to do things like this? How does care for God's creation draw you closer to him?

Part IV

Sin and Its Social Dimensions

Part IV: Chapter 1

WHAT IS SOCIAL SIN?

Memory Verse

> Temptations to sin are sure to come; but woe to him by whom they come! It would be better for him if a millstone were hung round his neck and he were cast into the sea, than that he should cause one of these little ones to sin.
>
> —LUKE 17:1–2

Key Terms

Social sin

Utilitarian

Materialism

Consumerism

Questions for Review

1. What does it mean to "cooperate with social sin"?

2. What does it mean to hold a "utilitarian" attitude?

3. What is materialism?

4. What is consumerism?

5. Give two reasons why pornography is a good example of social sin.

Quiz

1. Sin is __________ but not ___________.
2. The roots of social sin lie in attitudes or philosophies that ______________.
3. Those who have a _________ attitude see others in terms of their usefulness.
4. ____________ believe that only those things that can be empirically verified by science are real.
5. The first step to helping conquer social sin is to conquer ___________.

Questions for Discussion

1. Have you ever been guilty of treating someone in a utilitarian way? Explain.
2. What do you think materialism looks like in practice? Is this ever a temptation for you? Why or why not?
3. How does our culture promote consumerism? Explain. Why is this dangerous?

Essay Topics / Further Study

1. How does doing nothing or saying nothing in regards to social sin help spread it even more? How are we still promoting the sin even in our silence?
2. The text said that one of the best ways we can help combat social sin is to conquer our own personal sin. Do you agree with this? How could this be true? Can you give examples?
3. Imagine you have a friend who confides in you that he is addicted to pornography. How would you charitably counsel him while still conveying the evil of his actions? If it helps, write out a letter to him.

Part IV: Chapter 2

The Social Dimension of the Ten Commandments: The First Four Commandments

Memory Verse

> And God spoke all these words, saying, "I am the Lord your God, who brought you out of the land of Egypt, out of the house of bondage. You shall have no other gods before me."
>
> —Exodus 20:1–3

Key Terms

The first commandment

The second commandment

The third commandment

The fourth commandment

Worship

Disintegration

Idolatry

Questions for Review

1. What does it mean to worship God?

2. On a social level, to what actions do the first three commandments ask us to say yes?

3. On a social level, to what actions do the first three commandments ask us to say no?

4. On a social level, to what does the fourth commandment ask us to say yes?

5. On a social level, to what does the fourth commandment ask us to say no?

Quiz

True/False

1. ____ To be a Christian is to be a person in relationship with Jesus Christ.
2. ____ The first three commandments pertain to our relationship with our neighbor.
3. ____ Original sin can lead us to worship other things besides God, even if we say we worship him.
4. ____ Idolatry only consists in the worship of pagan gods.
5. ____ The commandment of honoring our fathers and mothers extends beyond just our biological fathers and mothers to include our teachers, priests, grandparents, etc.

Questions for Discussion

1. Who or what, besides God, are you tempted to worship?
2. In what ways are you tempted to say no to the first three commandments? Why? When you fail to say yes to God in these particular ways, what might some of the consequences be for you and for those around you?
3. What are some ways you've seen people disregard the social aspects of the fourth commandment? Describe. What do you think are the consequences of this disregard for both the individual and society?

Essay Topics / Further Study

1. How does it affect your view of the spiritual life when you simplify it down to just being in relation with Jesus and sharing a friendship with him? Is it truly as simple as saying yes to certain things he asks of us and no to those things that get in the way of that relationship? What things do you have trouble saying yes and no to?
2. Consider your daily life and ask yourself if there is anything that you place at the center of our happiness outside of God. Are you in danger of making this thing a false god? What specific actions can you take to overcome this temptation?
3. What things do you see in the culture at large that people tend to worship instead of worshipping God? What areas attract the most attention and pull souls away from God?
4. Why do you think sin often gives the feeling of being broken inside? What is it about sin that leads to this "disintegration," as the text mentioned?

Part IV: Chapter 3

THE SOCIAL DIMENSION OF THE TEN COMMANDMENTS: THE FIFTH COMMANDMENT

Memory Verse

> You have heard that it was said to the men of old, "You shall not kill; and whoever kills shall be liable to judgment." But I say to you that every one who is angry with his brother shall be liable to judgment; whoever insults his brother shall be liable to the council, and whoever says, 'You fool!' shall be liable to the hell of fire.
>
> —MATTHEW 5:21–22

Key Terms

The fifth commandment

Caritas in Veritate

Evangelium Vitae

Abortion

Euthanasia (active and passive)

Ordinary treatment

Extraordinary treatment

Cloning

Just war theory

Capital punishment

Scandal

Questions for Review

1. What does openness to life bring to a society? What are some of the consequences for a society that is closed to life?

2. Why is abortion contrary to the fifth commandment?

3. What is the difference between active and passive euthanasia? Is either ever permissible?

4. Under what conditions is a war considered just and not a violation of the fifth commandment?

5. What is the sin of scandal?

Quiz

1. A society that is not open to life leads to what kind of attitude?
   A. tough
   B. utilitarian
   C. petty
2. The best way to build a just society that respects the dignity of human life is by:
   A. pressuring politicians and people in power to pass laws that respect life.
   B. take up arms against those who do not respect life.
   C. love others as Christ loves us.
3. Under what circumstances is abortion permissible?
   A. In the case of rape.
   B. When the safety of the mother is in jeopardy.
   C. Abortion is never permissible.
4. Which of the following is an instance of passive euthanasia?
   A. pulling a patient off life support when he shows no signs of brain activity
   B. giving someone a lethal dose of morphine
   C. providing a lethal cocktail of drugs
5. Why is it important to not actively euthanize someone just because they are suffering?
   A. Because suffering can be spiritually beneficial to the one in pain and perhaps others as well.
   B. Because oftentimes breakthroughs in medical treatment occur when someone is willing to endure suffering.
   C. All of the above.
6. Why would long-term incarceration be preferred over the death penalty, or "capital punishment"?
   A. Because capital punishment is always wrong.
   B. Because it allows the criminal a chance to repent and make amends for their wrongdoing.
   C. Because capital punishment costs more tax money to carry out.
7. Whose writings are the Church's "just war theory" pulled from?
   A. St. Augustine
   B. Pope St. John Paul II
   C. Sacred Scripture
8. Which of the following is *not* one of the conditions that must be met for a war to be considered just?
   A. There must be a reasonable chance of success.
   B. All other options for peace must have been pursued.
   C. The nation which you have declared war against must be persecuting its citizens.

9. True or False: If a solider fighting in a just war is ordered by his superior officer to kill an unarmed prisoner, he must disobey the order.
   A. true
   B. false

10. Which of the following is *not* an example of the sin of scandal?
    A. mean thoughts about another person
    B. gossiping about another person with friends
    C. public drunkenness.

Questions for Discussion

1. Do you think we live in a culture of life or a culture of death? Explain.
2. How can you personally commit to helping build a culture of life?
3. Has your faith ever been shaken by the sin of scandal? Explain. What does this tell you about the importance of your own witness?

Essay Topics / Further Study

1. Imagine you have a friend who is against abortion but says it must be allowed in the case of rape or the safety of the mother. How would you explain the Catholic point of view on these issues to convince him or her that abortion is *never* permissible?
2. Imagine you have a friend who thinks someone should be allowed to die when they are suffering greatly in a hospital bed. How would you explain the Catholic point of view on euthanasia and teach this person the merits of suffering?
3. Imagine you are in the office of the president of the United States, and you are one of his chief counselors. He has to decide if the United States will wage war against a hostile nation. Go through the Church's "just war theory" conditions and explain what each of these are and what they mean, asking him if each is met.
4. What is your view of capital punishment? Do you think it should be allowed in rare cases? Do you think it is a good deterrent from crime? What arguments can you make to support your point of view? Do outside research if necessary.

Part IV: Chapter 4

The Social Dimension of the Ten Commandments: The Seventh, Eighth, and Tenth Commandments

Memory Verse

> I tell you, on the day of judgment men will render account for every careless word they utter; for by your words you will be justified, and by your words you will be condemned.
>
> —Matthew 12:36–37

Key Terms

The seventh commandment

The eighth commandment

The tenth commandment

False witness

Defamation

Detraction

Perjury

Slander

Questions for Review

1. What virtues are necessary for following the seventh and tenth commandments in a social context?

2. In a social context, to what do the seventh and tenth commandments require we say no?

3. What is the relationship between God and truth?

4. How can we say yes to the eighth commandment in a social context?

5. In a social context, to what does the eighth commandment require we say no?

Quiz

1. To honor the seventh and tenth commandments, we must avoid the sin of greed by welcoming a __________ life.

2. The eighth commandment states ______________________.

3. __________ is the source of all truth.

4. To say yes to the truth is to say yes to the __________.

5. Those who work in _____________ have an especially large duty to the truth.

Questions for Discussion

1. Of the five virtues we need to cultivate in order to follow the seventh and tenth commandments, which comes most naturally to you? What is more difficult? What is one habit you could start practicing to grow stronger in that difficult virtue?
2. What are some of the ways we can lie with our actions?
3. The Church teaches that the media—including musicians and filmmakers—has a responsibility to promote truth. Can you think of some ways the media does this? Can you think of some ways the media fails to do this?

Essay Topics / Further Study

1. What do you think it means to live a "simple life"? How would living a simple life keep you from breaking the seventh and tenth commandments?
2. The text told us that the true and the good go hand in hand. How do you reconcile this when sometimes the truth is difficult to accept or tell someone? Explain how even when the truth is hard, it still brings about the good. Can you give specific examples? Make them up or take some from your life.
3. What makes the sin of gossip so bad? Why is it so easy to engage in? What are specific acts you can take in your everyday life to guard against the sin of gossip?
4. What are the dangers of disinformation that spread through the news media and social media? How can this cause the breakdown of a culture? What can you do to guard your own life and mind against the spread of false information?

Part V

Sin and Its Social Dimensions, Continued

Part V: Chapter 1

The Social Dimension of the Ten Commandments: The Sixth and Ninth Commandments

Memory Verse

> You have heard that it was said, "You shall not commit adultery." But I say to you that every one who looks at a woman lustfully has already committed adultery with her in his heart.
>
> —Matthew 5:27–28

Key Terms

The sixth commandment

The ninth commandment

The sacrament of Matrimony

Consummation

Chastity

Contraception

Natural family planning (NFP)

Questions for Review

1. What are the five hallmarks of Catholic marriage?

2. What is chastity? How is it lived differently in different states in life?

3. What are the two ends of marriage?

4. What consequences did Pope Paul VI predict would follow from the widespread use of contraception?

5. What are the hallmarks of a virtuous friendship?

Quiz

True/False

1. ____ A sacramental Catholic marriage has several unique characteristics. These include exclusivity (no polygamy allowed), indissolubility until death (there is no such thing as a "Catholic divorce"), and continual openness to having children (contraception may not be used).
2. ____ The Church instituted marriage as a sacrament.
3. ____ Chastity can apply to married couples as well.
4. ____ For the Christian, love means making others happy and treating them kindly.
5. ____ Even after the Protestant Reformation, all Christians agreed that sex outside of marriage was immoral.
6. ____ Contraception can lead to dire consequences for the couple and for society at large.
7. ____ Contraception keeps unwanted pregnancies and abortions down.

8. ____ The Church teaches that there is no such thing as homosexual "marriage."
9. ____ Prayer and the sacraments will help us practice chastity, but we must also strengthen our own self-discipline.
10. ____ Chastity is a negative prohibition of sexuality.

Questions for Discussion

1. Describe one of the best marriages you have ever witnessed. What about it made it beautiful?
2. How accurate do you think Pope Paul VI was in his predictions about contraception? Explain.
3. What makes it difficult to practice chastity in our culture? What can we do to overcome those difficulties?

Essay Topics / Further Study

1. Write a letter to your future spouse about why it is important that you both save yourselves for marriage. Why do you think, outside of just keeping you holy, that it will benefit your marriage?
2. Why do you think a society is only as healthy as the health of its marriages? How do broken homes affect the culture at large?
3. Make a list of ten reasons why contraception is wrong and harmful, both physically and spiritually.

Part V: Chapter 2

The Social Dimension of the Beatitudes

Memory Verse

> Seeing the crowds, he went up on the mountain, and when he sat down his disciples came to him. And he opened his mouth and taught them, saying:
>
> "Blessed are the poor in spirit, for theirs is the kingdom of heaven.
> "Blessed are those who mourn, for they shall be comforted.
> "Blessed are the meek, for they shall inherit the earth.
> "Blessed are those who hunger and thirst for righteousness, for they shall be satisfied.
> "Blessed are the merciful, for they shall obtain mercy.
> "Blessed are the pure in heart, for they shall see God.
> "Blessed are the peacemakers, for they shall be called sons of God.
> "Blessed are those who are persecuted for righteousness' sake, for theirs is the kingdom of heaven.
> "Blessed are you when men revile you and persecute you and utter all kinds of evil against you falsely on my account. Rejoice and be glad, for your reward is great in heaven, for so men persecuted the prophets who were before you."

—Matthew 5:1–12

Key Terms

The Beatitudes

Poor in spirit

Meekness

Mercy

Pure in heart

Questions for Review

1. What does the word "beatitude" mean?

2. What is spiritual poverty?

3. Who are the meek?

4. What does it mean to show mercy?

5. What is promised to those who are persecuted for the sake of Christ?

Quiz

1. Happiness is:
   A. feeling good.
   B. material comfort.
   C. true and lasting satisfaction.
2. This beatitude is the alternative to thinking you are your own god:
   A. meekness.
   B. poverty of spirit.
   C. peacemaker.
3. This beatitude keeps us focused on God and we see him as the most important thing:
   A. meekness.
   B. those who hunger and thirst for righteousness.
   C. pure of heart.

4. Those who practice this beatitude are not concerned with worldly power, but are content with who they are, knowing all that matters is one's relationship with God:
   A. meekness.
   B. pure of heart.
   C. poverty of spirit.

5. Righteousness means:
   A. being kind.
   B. living out the will of god.
   C. defending the weak.

Questions for Discussion

1. Who are the spiritually poor in our culture?
2. Who is someone that has shown mercy to you? What did receiving mercy feel like? Is it easy or difficult for you to imitate them in showing mercy to others? Explain.
3. Have you ever been in a situation where if you stood up for what was right or did what was right, you would face persecution (being teased, rejected, or losing something you valued)? What did you do? Why?

Essay Topics / Further Discussion

1. Pick one of the beatitudes that interests you most to study further. What is the common understanding of what it means, and what is the deeper meaning? Where do you see this beatitude being practiced in our culture? Where do you see the opposite of this beatitude being practiced? How can you live out this beatitude in your everyday life?
2. Do outside research and write down the "anti-beatitude." What are these behaviors that conflict with the beatitudes? Where do you see them in society? Do you suffer from any of them?
3. The beatitudes are the most studied and discussed subject of Jesus's Sermon on the Mount. But he said many of significant things. Do outside research to discover three other important teaches from this sermon, and how they apply to your everyday life.

Part V: Chapter 3

The Two Great Commandments

Memory Verse

> But when the Pharisees heard that he had silenced the Sadducees, they came together. And one of them, a lawyer, asked him a question, to test him. "Teacher, which is the great commandment in the law?" And he said to him, "You shall love the Lord your God with all your heart, and with all your soul, and with all your mind. This is the great and first commandment. And a second is like it, You shall love your neighbor as yourself. On these two commandments depend all the law and the prophets."[i]
>
> —Matthew 22:34–40

Key Terms

The two great commandments

Philia

Eros

Storge

Agape

Questions for Review

1. What are the two greatest commandments Jesus gives us?

2. What are the four different types of love? Define each one.

3. What kind of love does Jesus show to us?

4. How did Christ demonstrate his love for us?

5. What did he leave us as a sign of his love for us?

Quiz

1. The two greatest commandments are ____________________.

2. The name for romantic love is ____________.

3. The name for the love we share with friends is _____________.

4. The name for the love we share with our family is ____________.

5. Jesus says that we must love everyone, even our ____________.

Questions for Discussion

1. Who is someone who has shown you sacrificial love? Explain.
2. Why is it difficult to love others?
3. Is it ever difficult for you to receive love from God and others? Explain. Why or why not?

Essay Topics / Further Study

1. When we hear Jesus say that you must love your neighbor "as yourself," what do you think he means? Are we not supposed to be humble and not always care about our needs and wants? Why would he want us to love ourselves?
2. Do research on those four different types of love: *eros*, *philia*, *storge*, and *agape*. What are the origins of these words and what do they mean? Explain how each of these loves differs from one another.

Final Exam ______ / 100

Matching

2 Points Each

A. Sermon on the Mount
B. Dualistic anthropology
C. Chastity
D. Justice
E. Corporal works of mercy
F. Paschal mystery
G. Beatitude
H. Consumerism
I. Subsidiarity
J. Trinity
K. *Rerum Novarum*
L. Moral law
M. Materialism
N. Baptism
O. Anthropology
P. Industrial Revolution
Q. Intrinsic human dignity
R. *Evangelium Vitae*
S. Spiritual works of mercy
T. Materialistic anthropology
U. The Church
V. Torah
W. The family
X. Hylomorphism
Y. Scandal

_____ 1. God's law
_____ 2. The passion, death, resurrection, and ascension of Jesus Christ
_____ 3. The concept that every human life matters
_____ 4. Our model for how we ought to live together in community
_____ 5. States that the human body is completely separate from and extraneous to the soul or mind.
_____ 6. How we become God's sons and daughters
_____ 7. The Catholic understanding of the human person which recognizes that we are body-soul composites and cannot be fully ourselves unless body and soul are united
_____ 8. The family of God
_____ 9. Ways we can serve the spiritual needs of our neighbor
_____ 10. The moral virtue that consists of giving God and others what is due to them
_____ 11. The Church's first social encyclical
_____ 12. Means "happiness"
_____ 13. The belief by which a community of a higher order should not interfere in the internal life of a community of a lower order
_____ 14. Provides the foundation for all social teaching
_____ 15. The attitude that sees the ability to purchase, use, and dispose of material things as the highest good in human life
_____ 16. Where Jesus preached about the Beatitudes
_____ 17. Ways we can serve the bodily needs of our neighbor
_____ 18. A social encyclical dedicated to the right to life
_____ 19. States that the world in general and human beings in particular are comprised solely of material elements that can be scientifically verified and measured
_____ 20. Radically changed the social and economic fabric of much of the world
_____ 21. An explanation of the nature of the human person
_____ 22. The foundation of all society
_____ 23. The belief that only things that can be empirically verified by science are worthy of belief (are "real")
_____ 24. A public sin that leads others into immoral behavior
_____ 25. The inner strength that enables us to integrate our sexual desires with our desire to love and be loved.

Short Answer

5 Points Each

1. Can we be perfectly happy on our own? Why or why not?

2. Describe two ways the behavior of the early Christians differed from their pagan neighbors.

3. What are the corporal works of mercy? What are the spiritual works of mercy?

4. How are all people equal? How are they not equal? When are inequalities good, and when are they bad?

5. What three principles inform all of the social encyclicals of the Church?

6. What basic rights of workers does the Church teach must be respected?

7. What does it mean to hold a "utilitarian" attitude?

8. What does openness to life bring to a society? What are some of the consequences for a society that is closed to life?

9. What is the difference between active and passive euthanasia? Is either ever permissible?

10. What are the five hallmarks of Catholic marriage?

Answer Key

Part I: Chapter 1—The Call of God

Questions for Review

1. What is the call of Jesus that is reflected in Catholic social teaching?

The call of Jesus reflected in Catholic social teaching is to express our love for him by loving others through concrete actions in society.

2. What is hell?

Hell is a place of eternal suffering and death.

3. Why do we need someone divine to save us?

We need someone divine to save us because we need someone who is not in the situation we are in, meaning someone who is not plagued by sin; we need someone who can forgive our sins—someone who is "outside" sin—and only a divine being can do this.

4. Why do we need someone human to save us?

All sacrifices require a material element. In the Old Testament, priests sacrificed animals, grain, and various other elements of creation. In this new covenant, Jesus himself is the sacrifice. He needed to be human to physically make the sacrifice of his life for our sins.

5. What is the paschal mystery?

The paschal mystery is the passion, death, resurrection, and ascension of Jesus Christ.

Quiz

True/False

1. False; the primary way to view the faith is to have a relationship with Jesus.
2. True
3. True
4. False; he took on the consequences in his death but transformed them through his resurrection.
5. True

Part I: Chapter 2—Happiness in this Life

Questions for Review

1. What does it mean that we are created in God's image?

When Scripture says in Genesis 1:27 that human beings are created in God's image, it means that we are created to participate in and share God's perfect, unconditional, self-giving, and eternal love. We were also created with and intellect and free wiil as a reflection of God's intellect and freedom.

2. Who is our model for how we ought to live together in community?

The Trinity is our model for how we ought to live together in community.

3. Can we be perfectly happy on our own? Why or why not?

No, we cannot be perfectly happy on our own because we were created by God, who is a community of Persons, therefore our happiness in this life requires communion with others, with God and with our neighbors.

4. How do we become God's sons and daughters?

We become God's sons and daughters through the sacrament of Baptism.

5. What is the most powerful encounter we can have with Jesus in this lifetime?

The most powerful encounter we can have with Jesus in this lifetime is through the Catholic Church and her sacraments.

Quiz

1. B
2. A
3. C
4. B
5. C

Part II: Chapter 1—The Church Has Always Stood for Charity and Justice

Questions for Review

1. What did the prophets urge the ancient Israelites to do?

The prophets urged the ancient Israelites to follow God's commandments, to love him and to love their neighbor, to be generous to the poor and to care for the sick, and to avoid sin.

2. Name three commandments from the Old Testament and describe how Jesus intensified each commandment.

See text section titled "Charity and Justice is the Teachings of Jesus."

3. Describe two ways the behavior of the early Christians differed from their pagan neighbors.

The concept of *intrinsic human dignity*—the idea that every person was created in the image of God and therefore has value by virtue of being human, rather than what their position was or what family they were born into—was completely foreign to the ancient Greeks and Romans. Only with the advent of Christianity did the value of each human life take on meaning. Without this, children were aborted if they had handicaps or defects, and in some cases, people were not considered a person worthy of rights until a certain age or status was reached. Furthermore, there was no unified moral system under the guidance of a religious faith like Christianity, which meant many grave evils took place (see text for many examples).

4. What are the corporal works of mercy?

The corporal works of mercy are charitable ways we can serve the *bodily* needs of our neighbor, such as feeding the hungry, giving drink to the thirsty, sheltering the homeless, clothing the naked, visiting the sick and imprisoned, and burying the dead.

5. What are the spiritual works of mercy?

The spiritual works of mercy are charitable ways we can serve the *spiritual* needs of our neighbor, such as instructing the ignorant (or admonishing the sinner), advising those in need of counsel, consoling those who mourn, comforting those who are suffering, forgiving those who have wronged us, bearing wrongs patiently, and praying for the living and the dead.

Quiz

1. add-ons / optional
2. *Torah*
3. prophets
4. Sermon on the Mount
5. outwardly
6. "Our Father"
7. how well we treated our neighbor
8. intrinsic human dignity
9. corporal
10. spiritual

Part II: Chapter 2—The Catholic Understanding of Justice

Questions for Review

1. What are the four types of justice? Name and give a short definition for each.

***Legal justice* is what each "citizen owes in fairness to the community" (CCC 2411), such as observing traffic laws and respecting the property of others. *Distributive justice* applies to the political realm. It is the responsibility of a government's authorities and the citizens who live under that government to ensure that each person has their share of common goods (for example, safe roads, clean water, and educational opportunities). *Commutative justice* refers to the regulation of "exchanges between persons and between institutions in accordance with a strict respect for their rights" (CCC 2411). This is the kind of justice required by a legal contract, and it means that each party upholds its end of the bargain in any exchange. Commutative justice also requires the "restitution of stolen goods to their owner" (CCC 2412). This means that "all who in some manner have taken part in a theft or who have knowingly benefited from it—for example, those who ordered it, assisted in it, or received the stolen goods—are obliged to make restitution in proportion to their responsibility and to their share of what was stolen" (CCC 2412). This is the most basic form of justice within a society because it is founded upon mutual trust and concern for the good of the other. Lastly, there is *social justice,* which is the responsibility of every individual that makes up a society: collectively, we are to provide the conditions that enable every person to receive what is due to them according to their nature and vocation (CCC 1928).**

2. What are three things political authorities owe to their citizens? What are three things citizen owe to political authorities?

See text under Distributive Justice subheading.

3. Are people obliged to obey immoral laws? Why or why not?

No, people must obey God's law first. If a civil law is immoral, citizens are not only not bound to follow it, they must disobey it.

4. What is the basis for all legitimate rights?

Social justice can only exist where respect for human dignity, given by God from the moment of conception, is encouraged and maintained. This dignity is the basis of all legitimate human rights, and without an understanding of human dignity, human rights have no underlying foundation; they are easily dismissed whenever they are inconvenient to those in power. This is why a lack of belief in this dignity inevitably leads to the most heinous crimes and abuses.

5. How are all people equal? How are they not equal? When are inequalities good, and when are they bad?

People are equal because they are all created in the image of God, giving them inherent dignity. But while all human beings possess equal dignity and are loved perfectly by God,

differences between particular persons continue to exist (age, health, physical or intellectual abilities, moral aptitude, etc.). These inequalities can serve an important purpose in God's providential design: they remind us that we need one another. No person, regardless of how talented, wealthy, or beautiful he or she is, can make it through life without the love and help of other people. Because of our differences, we are impelled not only to seek and welcome the generosity and kindness of others, but also to be generous and kind toward those we encounter who are in need of something that we have been given by God. Inequalities are *not* good when they are the result of sin, and therefore are unjust.

Quiz

True/False

1. True
2. False; the moral virtue that consists of giving God and others what is due to them.
3. True
4. False; Distributive justice
5. True
6. True
7. False; they *do* have duties to their citizens.
8. True
9. False; all three justices (commutative as well) must exist.
10. True

Part II: Chapter 3—Charity and Justice in the Modern Era

Questions for Review

1. What is considered the Church's first social encyclical? Who wrote it? When and why?

Pope Leo XIII's 1891 encyclical *Rerum Novarum* ("Of Revolutionary Change") was the Church's first social encyclical. He wrote it in response to the working and cultural changes that stemmed from the Industrial Revolution.

2. What social encyclical was written, in large part, to condemn racism and address issues surrounding the US civil rights movement? Who wrote this encyclical?

Pope St. John XXIII wrote *Pacem in Terris* ("Peace on Earth") to condemn racism, among other issues.

3. What social encyclical is dedicated to the right to life? Who wrote this encyclical?

John Paul II wrote *Evangelium Vitae* to address the right to life issue.

4. What are the social encyclicals of Pope Benedict XVI and Pope Francis?

In the wake of the 2008 international financial crisis, Pope Benedict XVI wrote a social encyclical in 2009 called *Caritas in Veritate* ("Charity in Truth"). In it, he calls for a Catholic

approach to issues such as global poverty, injustice, the arms race, the dangers of an increasingly technocratic world, and the need for holistic human development. He also calls for a greater concern and care for the environment. Most recently, Pope Francis issued his first social encyclical, *Laudato Si'* ("Praise Be to You"), in May of 2015. *Laudato Si'* is a comprehensive teaching on care for the environment that draws on social encyclicals by other modern popes (especially Pope St. John Paul II and Pope Benedict XVI) and addresses not only Catholics but all people of goodwill. In it, Pope Francis reminds us that care for the environment is a Christian obligation and that it is directly linked to social justice

5. What three principles inform all of the social encyclicals of the Church?

The three principles that inform all of the social encyclicals of the Church are: (1) The necessity of the moral law; that (2) God is the source of all civil authority; and (3) the perfection of the person by the common good.

Quiz

1. C
2. B
3. C
4. A
5. C
6. B
7. A
8. B
9. A
10. B

Part III: Chapter 1—The Cornerstone: The Dignity of Human Life

Questions for Review

1. What does the word "anthropology" mean?

Anthropology is an explanation of the nature of the human person.

2. What is a materialistic anthropology? What is a dualistic anthropology? What is wrong with both?

Materialistic anthropology states that the world in general and human beings in particular are comprised solely of material elements that can be scientifically verified and measured. Dualistic anthropology states that the human body is completely separate from and extraneous to the soul or mind. To dualists, the soul is the real person; the body is just matter, a thing apart from the soul and (usually) less important than the soul. Many dualists, in fact, see the entire material world as illusory and meaningless; for dualists, it is only the spiritual (or

mental) that matters. For her part, the Church rejects both materialism and dualism. She recognizes that both are inadequate anthropologies: materialism because it denies the spiritual dimension of the person (the soul), and dualism because it denies the essential connection between the body and soul.

3. What is hylomorphism?

The Catholic understanding of the human person is "hylomorphism," which recognizes that we are body-soul composites and cannot be fully ourselves unless body and soul are united.

4. What is the personalistic principle?

Human beings, the only creatures created in the image of God, are meant to be loved, not used. This is called the "personalistic principle." The personalistic principle reinforces the idea that every human being who has ever lived or will ever live is sacred because each of us is created and redeemed by God.

5. In what ways does the human person image God?

Being made in the image of God does not mean that we physically look like God but rather that we possess certain characteristics that set us apart from the rest of creation. A human person images God's spiritual nature in his or her immortal, rational soul (the spiritual principle of the person that can never die), specifically in the intellect (the ability to know) and in free will (the ability to choose the good and to love). It is when we exercise our free will by choosing to love others that we are most like God, who is love (1 John 4:16).

Quiz

1. Human dignity
2. animals
3. dualists
4. sacramental
5. sin

Part III: Chapter 2—Building Blocks

Questions for Review

1. What institution is the foundation of all society?

The family is the foundation of all society.

2. What are four things just governments must ensure for all men and women regarding the family?

The government should ensure the following for men and women:

- **the freedom to establish a family, have children, and bring them up in keeping with the family's own moral and religious convictions;**

- **the protection of the stability of the marriage bond and the institution of the family;**
- **the freedom to profess one's faith, to hand it on, and raise one's children in it, with the necessary means and institutions;**
- **the right to private property, to free enterprise, to obtain work and housing, and the right to emigrate;**
- **in keeping with the country's institutions, the right to medical care, assistance for the aged, and family benefits;**
- **the protection of security and health, especially with respect to dangers like drugs, pornography, alcoholism, etc.;**
- **the freedom to form associations with other families and so to have representation before civil authority [Cf. FC 46]. (CCC 2211)**

3. What makes for true community?

No matter what community we participate in, it is necessary, for the sake of human flourishing, that it is grounded in personal relationships and genuine care for the good of the other members. Each person in the community is a neighbor, "not a 'unit' in the human collective; he is 'someone' who by his known origins deserves particular attention and respect" (CCC 2212).

4. What are the three levels of participation in society to which each person is called?

The first level of participation in society is that of personal responsibility, such as the responsibility to fulfill our duties to our family, friends, fellow students, and coworkers. The second level of responsibility is public life. Each of us is called to participate in public life to the degree that is possible based on our age and position in society. Third, in order to participate in realizing the common good, each of us must continually seek conversion, asking Christ to give us more generous, loving, and self-sacrificing hearts.

5. Define "subsidiarity."

Subsidiarity is the belief by which a community of a higher order should not interfere in the internal life of a community of a lower order, depriving the latter of its functions, but rather should support it in case of need and help to co-ordinate its activity with the activities of the rest of society, always with a view to the common good [CA 48 §4; cf. Pius XI, Quadragesimo anno I, 184–186]. (CCC 1883)

Quiz

True/False

1. True
2. False; the family
3. True
4. False; it would go against subsidiarity if it was reversed (if the federal government sought to control the state governments)
5. True

Part III: Chapter 3—Essential Elements

Questions for Review

1. What does the Church mean by the phrase "preferential option for the poor"?

This phrase means we should put the needs of the poor and vulnerable first.

2. What is the "universal destination of goods"?

Pope John Paul II in his encyclical *Centesimus Annus*, coined the phrase "universal destination of goods on the earth." He argued that every good thing in the universe is a gift from God and does not "belong" in the strict sense to any one person or group of persons. Ownership of private property is still a human right and ought to be protected, as long as it is "acquired or received in a just way" (CCC 2403) and does not foster greed, possessiveness, or consumerism. Nevertheless, each person should see his or her private goods as gifts received from God and should be ready and willing to give them away or share them with those in need. For the same reason, we should consume our goods in moderation and save the best of what we have, not for ourselves, but for our guests, the sick, the poor, the homeless, the outcast, the unpopular, and the marginalized in our society. In doing so, we see and love Christ.

3. What basic rights of workers does the Church teach must be respected?

The basic rights of workers that must be respected include:

- **The right to productive work**
- **The right to decent and fair wages**
- **The right to the organization and joining of unions**
- **The right to private property**
- **The right to economic initiative**

4. What is solidarity?

Solidarity means that we are one human family regardless of our national, racial, ethnic, economic, and ideological differences. By virtue of the fact that we are all human beings created by the same God, we are responsible to and for one another. Accordingly, each of us has a responsibility to pursue justice and peace for all people, not simply those whose interests directly impact ours.

5. What is our obligation to creation?

We are stewards of creation and therefore have a right to use animals and plants as a means to help us survive, but we must always do so with moderation and a sense of respect for God's creations. We have an obligation to care for creation because it is a gift from God and because we must ensure future generations share in the same abundant blessings.

Quiz

1. B
2. C
3. A
4. C
5. A

Part IV: Chapter 1—What Is Social Sin?

Questions for Review

1. What does it mean to "cooperate with social sin"?

Cooperation with social sin can take the form of participating directly in evil, "ordering, advising, praising, or approving" of evil, not bringing structures of sin to light, not trying to stop evil from being done, or protecting those who do evil (CCC 1868).

2. What does it mean to hold a "utilitarian" attitude?

A utilitarian attitude means we see others only in regards to how we might use them for our gain (we only see their "utility"). This means those who are sick, weak, lame, or unintelligent serve no purpose.

3. What is materialism?

Materialism is the belief that only things that can be empirically verified by science—the *material* world—are worthy of belief (are "real").

4. What is consumerism?

Consumerism is the attitude that sees the ability to purchase, use, and dispose of material things as the highest good in human life. Consumerists don't recognize the needs of the poor, the concept of the universal destination of goods, or the fact that the most important realities are those that cannot be bought or sold.

5. Give two reasons why pornography is a good example of social sin.

Pornography is an example of social sin because it affects so many more people than just those who actively participate in the making or viewing of it. It ruins marriages and families, contributes to the sex trade, causes sexual violence, and cheapens the beauty of human sexuality. It can also have affects that last several generations.

Quiz

1. personal / private
2. foster unjust treatment of others
3. utilitarian
4. Materialists
5. personal sin

Part IV: Chapter 2—The Social Dimension of the Ten Commandments: The First Four Commandments

Questions for Review

1. What does it mean to worship God?

Worship is the submission, devotion, or offering of oneself entirely to something or someone. Worshipping God is acknowledging that everything, including our very existence, is a gift from God and that we owe him everything, including our very selves. This means our relationship with God takes precedence over all other relationships, activities, interests, and goals.

2. On a social level, to what actions do the first three commandments ask us to say yes?

- **Protecting and working for the right to religious freedom for all people**
- **Evangelizing others so that they may come to know the fullness of the truth communicated by Christ through the Church**
- **"Respect[ing] and awaken[ing] in each man the love of the true and the good" through our lived witness to the beauty of the Catholic faith (CCC 2105)**
- **Resting from unnecessary work, spending time with our families, and cultivating silence on Sundays**
- **Worshipping the Lord by participating in the Eucharistic liturgy (Mass) every Sunday and on holy days of obligation, unless one is sick or has a legitimate impediment to attending Mass**
- **Being especially mindful of the poor who are unable to rest from their labors, and doing what is within our means to help them**
- **Seeking "recognition of Sundays and the Church's holy days as legal holidays" (CCC 2188)**

3. On a social level, to what actions do the first three commandments ask us to say no?

- **Forcing anyone to convert or to believe in the Catholic faith (or any other religion)**
- **Forcing anyone to act against their conscience**
- **Worshipping the State**
- **Worshipping personal liberty**
- **Using God's name in a disrespectful way or disrespecting the name of any person**
- **Preventing others from enjoying rest or participating in worship on Sunday**
- **Skipping Mass on Sunday (unless you are sick or have a legitimate impediment)**

4. On a social level, to what does the fourth commandment ask us to say yes?

- **Respect for legitimate civil authority: even if we do not like or agree with those in public office, we still have an obligation to respect and obey them as long as they don't command something contrary to God's law.**
- **Government care for citizens' rights: government leaders must do what they can to safeguard the human rights of citizens, especially the rights of the most vulnerable (the unborn, poor, elderly, sick, imprisoned, refugees, etc.).**

- **Citizens' participation in public life: we must actively participate in society and in the political process, insofar as it's possible to do so without compromising the faith.**
- **Conscientious objection to unjust laws: the only time it is permissible to disobey those in authority over us is if they ask us to obey an unjust law or command. We must not obey unjust laws or be silent when those laws are passed or affirmed by our government leaders.**

5. On a social level, to what does the fourth commandment ask us to say no?

- **Anarchy (complete disrespect for all government authorities)**
- **Civil unrest**
- **Corrupt government**
- **Ignoring common good in order to pursue selfish goals**
- **Non-participation in democratic society, such as failing to vote due to laziness or failing to do your part in helping fight injustice on the political level**

Quiz

True/False

1. True
2. False; with God
3. True
4. False; we can worship things like money, sports, technology, etc. if we are placing them at the center of our lives rather than God
5. True

Part IV: Chapter 3—The Social Dimension of the Ten Commandments: The Fifth Commandment

Questions for Review

1. What does openness to life bring to a society? What are some of the consequences for a society that is closed to life?

Being open to life in a society strengthens its moral fiber and makes people capable of mutual help. By cultivating openness to life, wealthy peoples can better understand the needs of poor ones, they can avoid employing huge economic and intellectual resources to satisfy the selfish desires of their own citizens, and instead, they can promote virtuous action within the perspective of production that is morally sound and marked by solidarity, respecting the fundamental right to life of every people and every individual.

Without this openness to life and love for neighbor, societies all too quickly embrace utilitarian attitudes toward human life. As they do, those in power take it upon themselves to attach value to men and women based only on different qualities they possess, giving preference

to people based upon their usefulness, health, beauty, intelligence, influence, age, sex, race, nationality, or religion. From there, violations of human dignity follow. These violations are either accepted as "necessary" (abortion) or are seen as simply an exercise of human freedom (the use of pornography).

2. Why is abortion contrary to the fifth commandment?

Abortion is contrary the fifth commandment because it is the murder of a human life. From the moment of conception until the moment of natural death, each person possesses inviolable rights by virtue of being a human being created in the image of God. Killing a life just because it is still in the womb does not change the fact that it is a murder.

3. What is the difference between active and passive euthanasia? Is either ever permissible?

The difference between active and passive euthanasia is that with active you are purposely taking the life of someone who is sick or handicapped. This is always morally unacceptable. With passive euthanasia, there are degrees of moral acceptability. This involves a withdraw of treatments that is keeping the person alive. Any care given to the person that is considered "ordinary" (water, food, basic medications) should continue to be administered, and if it is not, then an immoral act has taken place. "Extraordinary" care goes beyond that of ordinary into experimental treatments or excessive and painful treatments that stand little chance of helping. In this case, one is not under an obligation to engage in these treatments for themselves or for a dying family member.

4. Under what conditions is a war considered just and not a violation of the fifth commandment?

A war is considered just if all chances for peace have been exhausted and a nation must defend itself against a hostile aggressor, and there is no international body that can step in. In this case, the Church asks those with the authority to declare war to consider the following criteria, first formulated by St. Augustine in the fourth century AD. Known collectively as "just war theory," each of these requirements must be met in order for a war to be considered just: (1) The damage inflicted by the aggressor on the nation or community of nations must be lasting, grave, and certain; (2) All other means of putting an end to it must have been shown to be impractical or ineffective; (3) There must be serious prospects of success; (4) The use of arms must not produce evils and disorders graver than the evil to be eliminated. The power of modern means of destruction weighs very heavily in evaluating this condition (CCC 2309).

5. What is the sin of scandal?

The sin of scandal is when we sin publicly and others are exposed to the sin and we lead others into this bad behavior.

Quiz

1. B
2. C
3. C

4. A
5. C
6. B
7. A
8. C
9. A
10. A

Part IV: Chapter 4—The Social Dimension of the Ten Commandments: The Seventh, Eighth, and Tenth Commandments

Questions for Review

1. What virtues are necessary for following the seventh and tenth commandments in a social context?

Generosity, responsibility, justice, stewardship, and simplicity.

2. In a social context, to what do the seventh and tenth commandments require we say no?

Stealing, damaging others' property, destruction to the environment, human trafficking, white-collar crime, violation of public trust by civil and governmental authorities, perpetuation of third-world poverty through the unjust economic practices of developed nations, and cultural attitudes that idealize wealth, such as consumerism and materialism.

3. What is the relationship between God and truth?

God is the source of truth.

4. How can we say yes to the eighth commandment in a social context?

Saying yes to the eighth commandment is saying yes to the truth, and therefore to the good, both for ourselves and our neighbors, and also society as a whole. This takes the form of speaking the truth in love to others, especially when it's difficult to do so. It means thinking before we speak and following through on our promises and commitments to others. It means that we resist, with the help of God's grace, the temptation to take the easy way out—lying or manipulating the truth to serve our selfishness. For Christians, saying yes to truth also means being faithful witnesses to the love of Christ and the truth of what he reveals in Scripture and Tradition.

5. In a social context, to what does the eighth commandment require we say no?

Saying yes to the eighth commandment means saying no to lying, detraction (speaking false ills of another), perjury, rash judgment, violation of confidentiality, and for priests, not breaking the seal of confession.

Quiz

1. simple/humble/generous
2. you shall not bear false witness against your neighbor
3. God
4. good
5. media/communications

Part V: Chapter 1—The Social Dimension of the Ten Commandments: The Sixth and Ninth Commandments

Questions for Review

1. What are the five hallmarks of Catholic marriage?

The five hallmarks of Catholic marriage:

- **Freely (love/sex are freely given, not forced)**
- **Fully (the gift is of the entire self)**
- **Faithfully (the gift of self is given to one person only)**
- **Fruitfully (the couple is always open to the possibility of new life)**
- **Until death (a sacramental marriage cannot be dissolved or ended by anything but death)**

2. What is chastity? How is it lived differently in different states in life?

The Catechism tells us that the virtue of chastity "means the successful integration of sexuality within the person" (CCC 2337). That is to say, chastity is the inner strength that enables us to integrate our sexual desires with our desire to love and be loved. Chasity can be carried out differently depending on what state of life we lead; for example, a priest will live a complete and total life of chastity, while being chaste in marriage means respecting the fullness of the Church's teachings on married love. Chastity for married people requires avoiding any lustful thoughts or actions, meaning we cannot use others—even our spouse—as a mere means of experiencing sexual pleasure. For single people (regardless of sexual orientation), chastity means recognizing sexual intimacy as an expression of love between a married man and woman that is intended to bond the couple and to produce new life. This means that any activity that is sexually arousing should be avoided if you're not married. Chastity for single people also means avoiding any lustful thoughts or actions.

3. What are the two ends of marriage?

The two ends of marriage are the procreation of children and the bonding of the couple.

4. What consequences did Pope Paul VI predict would follow from the widespread use of contraception?

Pope Paul VI predicted four major social consequences if contraception became widely available: (1) An increase in marital infidelity and a general lowering of morality; (2) a decline in respect for women; (3) growing coercive control by governments over sexuality; (4) people beginning to treat their own bodies as if there are no limits to what they may do

5. What are the hallmarks of a virtuous friendship?

A virtuous friendship is one in which both people care about each other's true happiness more than they care about their own desires. Virtuous friendships are oriented toward a common and greater goal than simply having fun. These are the friends who love you unconditionally, who challenge you to become the person God created you to be, who affirm your dignity as a person. None of us can be chaste on his or her own; we need good friends to encourage us to grow in virtue, to support us in our commitment to becoming men and women who love properly, and to help us fight the temptations to lust presented to us every day by the surrounding culture.

Quiz

1. True
2. False; Christ did
3. True
4. False; it means willing the good of the other (even if that doesn't make them happy or isn't "kind")
5. True
6. True
7. False; these things have actually increased since contraception has become more widespread
8. True
9. True
10. False; it is *not*

Part V: Chapter 2—The Social Dimension of the Beatitudes

Questions for Review

1. What does the word "beatitude" mean?

Beatitude means "happiness."

2. What is spiritual poverty?

Spiritual poverty is a recognition of our need for God, that we have nothing and are nothing without him.

3. Who are the meek?

The meek are those who are not addicted to power, and are content with who they are and what they have.

4. What does it mean to show mercy?

To show mercy is to do for others what Christ did for all of us, that is, to show forgiveness (even when it is not asked for) and to relinquish the debt one might owe us.

5. What is promised to those who are persecuted for the sake of Christ?

The persecuted will be given the Kingdom of Heaven.

Quiz

1. C
2. B
3. C
4. A
5. B

Part V: Chapter 3—The Two Great Commandments

Questions for Review

1. What are the two greatest commandments Jesus gives us?

The two greatest commandments are to love God with all of your heart, soul, and mind, and love your neighbor as yourself.

2. What are the four different types of love? Define each one.

The four different types of love are: (1) *philia* (friendship love), (2) *eros* (romantic love), (3) *storge* (family love), and (4) *agape* (selfless).

3. What kind of love does Jesus show to us?

Jesus shows us *agape* love, meaning it is entirely selfless and faithful.

4. How did Christ demonstrate his love for us?

He demonstrated his love for us by caring for the sick and poor, loving sinners, and dying on the cross.

5. What did he leave us as a sign of his love for us?

He left us his Real Presence—Body, Blood, Soul, and Divinity—in the Eucharist as a sign of his love.

Quiz

1. to love God and to love your neighbor as yourself
2. *eros*
3. *philia*
4. *storge*
5. *enemies*

Final Exam

Matching

1. V
2. F
3. Q
4. J
5. B
6. N
7. X
8. U
9. S
10. D
11. K
12. G
13. I
14. L
15. H
16. A
17. E
18. R
19. T
20. P
21. O
22. W
23. M
24. Y
25. C

Short Answer

1. Can we be perfectly happy on our own? Why or why not?

No, we cannot be perfectly happy on our own because we were created by God, who is a community of Persons, therefore our happiness in this life requires communion with others, with God and with our neighbors.

2. Describe two ways the behavior of the early Christians differed from their pagan neighbors.

The concept of *intrinsic human dignity*—the idea that every person was created in the image of God and therefore has value by virtue of being human, rather than what their position was or what family they were born into—was completely foreign to the ancient Greeks and Romans. Only with the advent of Christianity did the value of each human life take on meaning. Without this, children were aborted if they had handicaps or defects, and in some cases, people were not considered a person worthy of rights until a certain age or status was reached. Furthermore, there was no unified moral system under the guidance of a religious faith like Christianity, which meant many grave evils took place (see text for many examples).

3. What are the corporal works of mercy? What are the spiritual works of mercy?

The corporal works of mercy are charitable ways we can serve the *bodily* needs of our neighbor, such as feeding the hungry, giving drink to the thirsty, sheltering the homeless, clothing the naked, visiting the sick and imprisoned, and burying the dead.

The spiritual works of mercy are charitable ways we can serve the *spiritual* needs of our neighbor, such as instructing the ignorant (or admonishing the sinner), advising those in need of counsel, consoling those who mourn, comforting those who are suffering, forgiving those who have wronged us, bearing wrongs patiently, and praying for the living and the dead.

4. How are all people equal? How are they not equal? When are inequalities good, and when are they bad?

People are equal because they are all created in the image of God, giving them inherent dignity. But while all human beings possess equal dignity and are loved perfectly by God, differences between particular persons continue to exist (age, health, physical or intellectual abilities, moral aptitude, etc.). These inequalities can serve an important purpose in God's providential design: they remind us that we need one another. No person, regardless of how talented, wealthy, or beautiful he or she is, can make it through life without the love and help of other people. Because of our differences, we are impelled not only to seek and welcome the generosity and kindness of others but also to be generous and kind toward those we encounter who are in need of something that we have been given by God. Inequalities are *not* good when they are the result of sin, and therefore are unjust.

5. What three principles inform all of the social encyclicals of the Church?

The three principles that inform all of the social encyclicals of the Church are: (1) The necessity of the moral law; that (2) God is the source of all civil authority; and (3) the perfection of the person by the common good.

6. What basic rights of workers does the Church teach must be respected?

The basic rights of workers that must be respected include:

- **The right to productive work**
- **The right to decent and fair wages**
- **The right to the organization and joining of unions**
- **The right to private property**
- **The right to economic initiative**

7. What does it mean to hold a "utilitarian" attitude?

A utilitarian attitude means we see others only in regards to how we might use them for our gain (we only see their "utility"). This means those who are sick, weak, lame, or unintelligent serve no purpose.

8. What does openness to life bring to a society? What are some of the consequences for a society that is closed to life?

Being open to life in a society strengthens its moral fiber and makes people capable of mutual help. By cultivating openness to life, wealthy peoples can better understand the needs of poor ones, they can avoid employing huge economic and intellectual resources to satisfy the selfish desires of their own citizens, and instead, they can promote virtuous action within the perspective of production that is morally sound and marked by solidarity, respecting the fundamental right to life of every people and every individual.

Without this openness to life and love for neighbor, societies all too quickly embrace utilitarian attitudes toward human life. As they do, those in power take it upon themselves to attach value to men and women based only on different qualities they possess, giving preference to people based upon their usefulness, health, beauty, intelligence, influence, age, sex, race, nationality, or religion. From there, violations of human dignity follow. These violations are either accepted as "necessary" (abortion) or are seen as simply an exercise of human freedom (the use of pornography).

9. What is the difference between active and passive euthanasia? Is either ever permissible?

The difference between active and passive euthanasia is that with active you are purposely taking the life of someone who is sick or handicap. This is always morally unacceptable. With passive euthanasia, there are degrees of moral acceptability. This involves a withdraw of treatments that is keeping the person alive. Any care given to the person that is considered "ordinary" (water, food, basic medications) should continue to be administered, and if it is not, then an immoral act has taken place. "Extraordinary" care goes beyond that of ordinary

into experimental treatments or excessive and painful treatments that stand little chance of helping. In this case, one is not under an obligation to engage in these treatments for themselves or for a dying family member.

10. What are the five hallmarks of Catholic marriage?

The five hallmarks of Catholic marriage:

- **Freely (love/sex are freely given, not forced)**
- **Fully (the gift is of the entire self)**
- **Faithfully (the gift of self is given to one person only)**
- **Fruitfully (the couple is always open to the possibility of new life)**
- **Until death (a sacramental marriage cannot be dissolved or ended by anything but death)**